terrarium imaginarium

terrarium imaginarium

Growing succulents, cacti and more under glass

Isabelle Palmer

CICO BOOKS
LONDON NEW YORK

To my Grandmother, my guiding light

First published in 2014 as *The House Gardener*.
This edition published in 2023 by CICO Books
An imprint of Ryland Peters & Small Ltd
20–21 Jockey's Fields   341 E 116th St
London WC1R 4BW   New York, NY 10029

www.rylandpeters.com

10 9 8 7 6 5 4 3 2 1

A CIP catalog record for this book
is available from the Library of
Congress and the British Library.

ISBN: 978 1 80065 218 7

Printed in China

Copy editor: Caroline West
Photography: Helen Cathcart
Cover illustrations: AdobeStock
Stylist: Marisa Daly

In-house editor: Martha Gavin
Designer: Emily Breen
Art director: Sally Powell
Production: David Hearn
Publishing manager: Penny Craig
Publisher: Cindy Richards

FSC
www.fsc.org
MIX
Paper from
responsible sources
FSC® C106563

CONTENTS

INTRODUCTION

Living in the city, I am very aware that outdoor space is at a premium. However, with succulents, cacti, and other indoor plants becoming increasingly popular, it is now easier than ever to bring some greenery inside your home. Cacti and succulents thrive in indoor settings, and can look beautiful displayed in unusual terrariums and alternative glass containers. Not only that, but they are super low maintenance, and can become a real focal point of the room!

Even if you live in the country, indoor plants can offer some much-needed contact with nature, something that is so important, not only in terms of esthetics, but also to promote a healthy emotional environment. Houseplants bring their natural form, color, and fragrance to the home, and can add the finishing touch to many interior schemes.

Historically, plants have been used indoors for centuries—indeed, medieval paintings depict Crusaders returning with plant specimens from many corners of the world. The Victorian period in the nineteenth century was a golden age of plant collecting, which went hand in hand with the Victorians' passion for exploration and discovery. The Victorian plant hunters were seen as adventurers traveling to remote areas to bring back exotic plants from around the world. This era also saw a rise in popularity of terrariums and Wardian cases. The legacy of these Victorian plant explorers lives on in the plants that thrive in our modern natural landscape.

In this book, I will show you how to choose, grow, and decorate with houseplants, as well as guide you through the different techniques needed to care for your new "green guests."

There is nothing more pleasing than bringing greenery into your home. Not only are plants beautiful but many can clean household air and balance humidity.

1
SUCCULENTS, CACTI, AND PERENNIALS

One of the many joys of growing and displaying houseplants is being able to create your own living landscape or miniature garden. Glass vessels are exceptional in allowing you to watch, as well as house, your new living worlds. In this chapter, I have used various glass objects to encase and display an array of succulents, cacti, and other miniature houseplants, showing them off to their full glory. From angular terrariums and large glass vases to copper lanterns and wine glasses, let your imagination run riot when thinking of ways to display plant-based creations.

ENCLOSED IN GLASS

The word succulent is a descriptive term given to those plants that store water in their leaves or stems. Cacti belong to a large family of plants that are all succulents. There are also other types of succulent besides cacti. So, as a rule, remember that all cacti are succulents, but not all succulents are cacti.

The word "cactus" is derived, through Latin, from the Ancient Greek (*kaktos*), a name that was originally used to describe a spiny plant whose identity is now uncertain.

Succulents are found in many countries all over the world and have been a feature of the horticultural field for hundreds of years. They have always held an attraction for gardeners because of their curious and exotic appearance.

During the 15th century, the famous Portuguese explorers Bartholomeu Dias (1451–1500) and Vasco da Gama (1460–1524) collected succulents such as *Aloe, Haworthia, Stapelia,* and many others from Africa. They also discovered *Caralluma* and *Euphorbia* (spurge) in India during exploratory trips to find new trade routes to that country.

The Dutch East India Company (which was established in 1602) was also responsible for collecting many succulent species for the Dutch government. Many of these succulents also found their way to the world-famous Royal Botanical Gardens at Kew, in London.

DESERT HEARTH

If you're lucky enough to have an original fireplace, but don't have time to light a regular fire, then this handsome selection of cacti is for you. Of course, you don't need a fireplace to enjoy this display since an empty corner, or perhaps an unnoticed spot by the stairs, would work equally well. This display sits in a selection of beautiful copper lanterns. Rather helpfully, the cacti and succulents are all easy to care for and very low maintenance: they live well regardless of being in the shade and receiving just a little water—making them perfect plants for the novice or occasionally lazy gardener! (For further advice on caring for cacti and succulents, see page 125.)

The striking *Echinocactus grusonii* (golden barrel cactus) in the smaller black lantern is armed with stout, golden-yellow spines arranged carefully in rows on ribbed stems; it is quite the attention-seeker. You may find that it's sometimes known as the golden ball or, rather cheekily, as mother-in-law's cushion. I think it is one of the most distinctive of all cacti, and it is often used in architectural gardening due to its spherical shape.

Cacti can often be quite severe plants, but I find that *Mammillaria crinita* (rose pincushion cactus), seen in the larger dark lantern, is absolutely lovely. It's another spherical cactus and covered in regularly arranged yellow and brown spines. There are numerous reddish-purple flowers, which form a dense ring at the top. Also featured in this display is an *Aloe haworthioides* sitting tightly in a clay pot. This perennial succulent has lush, glossy leaves and small, rosette-like flowers. I also used gravel and reindeer moss in the display, as well as vintage medicine bottles.

NEAT ANGULARITY

I had this angular terrarium made for me as I was immediately drawn to a similar one I found online. Before I received it, I knew it would make a really unusual addition to the other terrariums in my collection. So many terrariums are tall and square, but this is something completely different. This quirky glasshouse, which is sat on its side, is visible from all angles and so is a great terrarium for a side table.

I knew that the lush, dark green moss, which is called 'Cushion,' would look really attractive from all viewing points, and planted the lovely, bright green leaves of oregano on top. I placed another of my finds from the doll house furniture shop—the miniature blue clock—at the edge of the entrance to the terrarium. This is what I love most about creating terrarium scenes: adding small pieces of detail and color in hidden corners.

CLASSIC SIMPLICITY

Lush, green succulents, assorted pebbles, and a terrarium on its side: such a simple and classic look, but it works really well. This small terrarium would add interest to a corner or side table, perhaps on a shelf in your bathroom? (For further advice on caring for cacti and succulents, see page 125.)

I love the clean lines and architectural form of this terrarium. The display inside emulates the beauty of a lotus leaf floating in a sea of pebbles and stone. The vivid greens of the succulents are striking and draw your attention to how truly glorious these plants are.

TALL & ELEGANT

This display is a wonderful example of how different textures and colors can work exceptionally well together. The delicate glass of the tall vase is offset beautifully by the weathered terracotta pot. You wouldn't automatically expect it, but the vase and pot work very well next to each other. This wine-glass terrarium is another example of how thinking imaginatively can be so successful when you are designing a terrarium display. Terrariums need not be vintage cases or steel-framed boxes—a dramatically shaped glass vase such as this will provide a beautiful home for your plants.

The bright yellow flowers of *Craspedia globosa* (bachelor's buttons) are akin to champagne bubbles floating to the top of a glass. They are bright and glossy, and just a few here and there create a wonderful picture; too many of them would be overkill.

Alongside the bachelor's buttons, I used a mossy green *Selaginella apoda* and a purple-flowered *Passiflora* (passionflower) to provide a lush green backdrop for the yellow bachelor's buttons and brown bark. You will need to keep the passionflower trimmed back as it grows so that it doesn't swamp the container.

In the antique terracotta pot, I planted peach-colored Tom Thumb (a hybrid of *Kalanchoe blossfeldiana*), which is a lovely, brightly colored plant that matches the weather-worn orange clay pot.

Previous pages: these three differently shaped wine glasses are perfect for bringing added detail to the main wine-glass display. Here, I used small pieces of different succulents, as well as some bun moss, to create a little world of interest. You can place a few pebbles in the base of the wine glasses to provide extra drainage, but, as long as you remember that these plants don't require lots of water, they should be fine. I have not included any potting mix here, but the succulents should last as long as the moss is kept moist.

BRIMFUL WITH SUCCULENTS

This stylish display is a must for the "I wish I had more time!" gardener, the "I always forget to water the plants" gardener, or simply the lazy gardener.

Succulents are the plants of the moment, and with such a range of shapes, colors, sizes and textures, it is easy to create a really interesting-looking display that is both low maintenance and beautiful.

In the past, succulents have been judged unfairly. Unfortunately, for some people they can conjure up images of sad, lonely plants in bathrooms, childhood gifts, or bad Mexican restaurants. But nowadays more and more people are falling in love with the odd shapes, the fleshy leaves, and the unusual colors, and I think they make very modern and stylish interior plants. They are minimalist plants with simple, streamlined shapes, and easily add a "desert chic" look to any home.

It can be a lot of fun putting together a succulent display—you can definitely include the weird and the wonderful here. I chose a selection of my favorites, including *Crassula ovata* (jade or money plant), *Sempervivum tectorum* (common house-leek or hens-and-chicks), *Aloe* 'Pinto,' *Sedum, Kalanchoe thyrsiflora* (paddle plant), *Epipremnum aureum* (devil's ivy), *Echeveria* 'Fred Ives,' *Crassula perforata* (string of buttons), and *Pachyveria glauca* 'Little Jewel,' along with *Lithops* (living stones or stone plant) and neutral pebbles. I painted the bowl a dark slate color, which I think offsets the overall look very well. (For further advice on caring for succulents, see page 125.)

The intricate beauty and delicacy of these fantastic
succulent plants are set off to perfection by the
surrounding stones.

EMPEROR OF ALL CACTI

This delicate terrarium is a nod to the Far East, with the dark potting mix on the base being a great support to—as well as a color contrast with—the small, pale gravel on top. I selected an array of cacti and succulents, including *Echinocereus pulchellus*, *Opuntia monstrosus*, and *Myrtillocactus geometrizans*, for this arrangement. The spikes and shapes of the plants are almost architectural. The plant shapes are all different, and I've left enough space around each plant so that they're not overcrowded. This terrarium reminds me of a delicate Japanese garden, ordered and structured.
(For further advice on caring for cacti and succulents, see page 125.)

ROCKY ROAD

This handsome trio of glass terrariums features an eclectic selection of different cacti, stones, and green mosses. Cacti hark back to an open, desert landscape—the final frontier. Here, they are captured in three beautiful open glass vases. (For further advice on caring for cacti and succulents, see page 125.)

Attractive glass vases are easy to source from homeware and interior shops, but it's a good idea to shop around to find vases that you particularly like and which will work in your indoor space. Think about where you want to put them, how much space you have, and how much light the space receives.

The three vases pictured overleaf are all different shapes and sizes, but still work well as a single display. Don't be afraid of placing terrariums and vases next to each other. Inside the vases is a selection of different pebbles that I collected from walks on the beach. Try to choose pebbles with different colors and textures that will contrast well. Pretty shells can also look striking in glass displays. If fact, picking shells and pebbles that can be used in a vase or terrarium once you return home can be a fun family holiday activity. I also found some pieces of granite and dried moss, which I used in the display to create different pockets of interest.

In the cylindrical vase, I used floristry sheet moss, which is lined with paper, making it easier to cut and shape to fit inside containers. This lush green moss looks wonderful, its lovely, bright, solid color creating a wonderful juxtaposition with the desert-like appearance of the other vases. The accents of fossils and small *Lithops* (stone plants) are a nod to archeological discovery. Finally, I added a beautiful turquoise gemstone to represent a blue pond surrounded by glistening rocks.

EXOTIC COCKTAIL

Cocktails on a Friday night are always something to look forward to after a particularly long, tiring week. This fun and flirty display is a celebration of the cocktail. It's a heady mix of both color and structure, and—like all good cocktails—it is a real attention-grabber. You can't be nervous about this plant display; it needs to be put in a prominent position for all to admire.

Rather wonderfully, the tall plants in the center of the vase are a type of pitcher plant known as *Sarracenia leucophylla*, which, for me, are a comical reminder of those sugary cocktails served in large pitchers. Not so here, however. In this display, the pitcher plants are elegant and sculptural. You need to be careful, though, as pitcher plants are carnivorous, featuring a deep cavity filled with liquid, which is known as a pitfall trap, for capturing hapless insects. Although this may sound ominous, the plants pictured are dormant and pose no risk (yet!) to passing flies or little fingers.

Pitcher plants prefer boggy, humid environments, so make sure that the potting mix remains constantly moist. Rather than using tap water, it's advisable to use distilled water or rainwater, or perhaps water collected from condensation, even from an air-conditioner. I also recommend planting pitcher plants in a soil-less potting mix, combining one part peat-substitute with one part sterilized sand. I put a layer of bark chips on top of the potting mix to help retain moisture. Pitcher plants also need plenty of sun, so be sure to place them in an area that receives at least six to eight hours of direct sunlight each day in summer.

Surrounding the pitcher plants are handsome *Viola* x *wittrockiana* (pansies), pretty little flowers, which, in this case, are a beautiful deep color. Pansies are a large group of plants, available in many colors, that are the result of a cross between two wild violets, and are said to attract love!

This glass container is striking in its majestic beauty. Standing tall and proud, it is an effortlessly chic arrangement that hints at delicious cocktail flavors.

SMALL BUT SWEET

One of my personal favorites, this terrarium presents a sweet picture with its tiny terracotta pots surrounded by tiny pebbles and tiny leaves. This is an easy terrarium to start with because the open top ensures that it's easy to add the potting mix and pebbles. The small, abundant leaves of the *Portulacaria afra* (miniature jade plant or elephant's food) also ensure that there is a splash of color. The size and shape of this terrarium are so different from the others in my collection. I found the little pieces of pottery in my favorite doll house furniture shop and housed them in here. These delicate pieces look lovely next to the tiny leaves of the plant. It's a three-dimensional display, so you can look at it from all angles.

MONOCHROME DESERT

Pebbles and stones look great in terrariums; they are available in lots of different shapes, sizes, and colors. You can mix and match as many as you want to create a busy picture, or build up a solid "block look" using stones of the same size and color. On a practical note, the stones are also useful for keeping the plants in place. Here, I contrasted the color of the smaller white pebbles with the dark potting mix—the monochrome look works really well, particularly when placed against a block neon colour such as pink. I found some small, lush plants, including a rosemary vine and *Sedum rubrotinctum*, which is often called the jelly bean plant, for this terrarium and surrounded them with smaller cacti in order to create a cool picture of a modern desert.

The pale hue of these stones, combined with the sage-green leaves, creates a delicate, but arresting, display.

TROPICAL SANCTUARY

A long soak in the bath is a wonderful opportunity for some "me" time in a busy life, and, not only that, but bathrooms make wonderful backdrops for indoor plants, as they are often flooded with light and the bright spaces allow the plants to shine.

The succulents and bright fleshy plants in this wonderfully dark arrangement all thrive in the warm surroundings of a bathroom. These plants also all retain moisture well and boast a beautiful depth of color.

One of my favorites is the tall *Maranta leuconeura* (prayer plant) with its stunning combination of colors that are set off by the dark clay pot. The patterns and coloring of this plant's leaves easily make it one of the most attractive plants in any arrangement you might put together. I have also discovered that the leaves of prayer plants partially fold up at night, just like hands at prayer!

The dark green *Aloe haworthioides* is a really luxuriant plant and has a fantastically wonderous look with its spiky fleshy leaves. It is a great plant for a bathroom and easily grows in full sun to partial shade. It flowers in late summer and early fall and has a beautifully delicate apricot color with a delicious sweetness to its fragrance. *Aloe haworthioides* is named for the resemblance to its cousins in the genus *Haworthia*. This resemblance is not a coincidence: *Aloe* and *Haworthia* are genetically close and they hybridize easily.

You should be careful for whom you buy the comically named mother-in-law's tongue! It is perhaps more diplomatic to call it by its botanical name—*Sansevieria trifasciata*. This is a dense, succulent perennial with stiff, sharp, evergreen leaves.

A stunning combination of different leaf shapes and colors really makes this bathroom arrangement stand out from the crowd.

A delicate heart-shaped fern is
enhanced wonderfully by the warmth
of the small terracotta vessel.

MEDITERRANEAN MEMORIES

Deep orange terracotta reminds me of vacations in Spain or Greece—as soon as you glance at the rich clay of a terracotta pot, you're instantly transported to sunny climes with the holiday sun shining on your face. This striking, globe-like terracotta pot makes a wonderfully simple container for *Hemionitis arifolia* (heart fern), a glossy green plant with heart-shaped leaves. Heart ferns grow to 6in (15cm) in height, making them perfect for growing in terrariums. They need shade and a well-drained potting mix.

COLOR SPLASH

Neon colors are startling and fresh in the modern home. An instant hit of color automatically lifts any interior—and is perfect for a white-toned room. I chose two solid, round zinc planters and carefully painted a neon-red strip around the top with paint bought at my local craft shop. I then chose two green succulents (*Aeonium urbicum* dinner plate and *crassula*) and planted them in the center of the pots—a simple, easy-to-create look, but one that boasts both style and an injection of color.

   I love the simplicity of this project. Using plants with different forms, but with the same color tone, will allow them to shine. One of the most interesting features of this display, along with the unusual textures and shapes, is the juxtaposition between the fresh green of the plants and the vibrant red of the pots.

2

TERRARIUMS AND WATER SCENES

Discovering vintage terrariums and using unexpected objects as containers is a wonderful and inventive way to show off and exhibit houseplants. In this chapter, I have collected a wealth of unusual containers to hold botanical displays. From mason jars to carboy bottles, and even old light bulbs, there is always a way to update and recycle unwanted objects.

The most rewarding aspect of using old finds for plant displays is the search—I love nothing better than trawling through antiques markets or junk shops, hunting for suitable containers. With a little effort, you can easily bring them up to scratch and create a truly unique spectacle.

THE GRASS
IS ALWAYS GREENER...

This striking, thick green glass dome makes a wonderful house for a plant display. The narrower neck and thicker glass keep the heat inside the dome— if using a terrarium made from thick glass, bear this in mind and select plants that thrive in warm, moist conditions. The dark soil here is a great base for the green moss, *Fittonia* (nerve plant), and array of ferns.

I found this carboy terrarium in a small craft shop and was immediately drawn to it as I remember my mother having one when I was small. They were very popular in the 1970s, and many came with a large cork stopper to seal the top of the terrarium. It's so different from all the other terrariums in my collection and I just loved its simple, curved lines.

The Boston fern and *Fittonia* create lots of interesting textures, which can be glimpsed through the wonderful green glass. This is a lovely, simple terrarium that boasts a warm, rustic feel.

Gloriously green in color, this stunning glass terrarium can be set off by a wonderful array of ferns or fittonias to create a lush landscape.

MESSAGE IN A BOTTLE

I love the idea of finding a missing bottle on the beach—perhaps an old, discarded bottle that contains a note for a loved one. This may be a romantic notion, but it makes a lovely starting-point for a terrarium story.

Whenever I visit antiques shops and vintage markets, I'm always sure to pick up a few old bottles as well. They're just so useful to have in stock for different planting and craft projects. This cobalt-blue bottle is an old find and I had popped it at the back of a kitchen cupboard.

When I started on this handsome terrarium, I knew I wanted to tell a story and was reminded of the old bottle sitting in my kitchen. Again, the wonderfully dark potting mix makes a great base for the picture and contrasts so well with the pale, round stones. I built up the tall green plants—here, I used an *Adiantum* (maidenhair fern) and a *Chamaedorea elegans* (parlour palm)—so that they would take up most of the space inside; they have such lush and vibrant leaves. Finally, I placed the lost bottle on the stones and, automatically, the terrarium tells a story.

There is a sense of wonder about this terrarium, giving you the feeling that you're looking into a hidden world or that there is perhaps a secret waiting to be discovered among the handsomely splayed leaves, which seem to be dancing around inside their enclosure.

Write a secret wish on a tiny piece of paper and hide it in a blue bottle for someone special to see.

AQUATIC DREAM

This small water garden (see left and opposite) is weighted down with large pebbles and rocks, which remind me of a rugged coastline. Indeed, I collected many of these stones on a recent trip to the Cornish coast. Looking after my terrariums has turned me into something of a magpie; I'm always looking for little items that can be used in a project. I chose a couple of different green water plants, namely *Myriophyllum* (water milfoil) and *Alternanthera*, which I knew would look lovely against the ashen color of the stones. The pretty clematis flower was picked from the garden to decorate the scene; it looks like a cool blue water lily floating on the surface of the water. (For further advice on aquatic horticulture, see page 113.)

In the glass container shown above left, I used *Fittonia argyroneurai*, *Echinodorus* 'Red Special,' and an aquatic fern. I weighed down the plants using some pebbles. This glorious red-hued display creates a very sophisticated look on the mantelpiece.

Water-themed containers are guaranteed to bring peace and serenity to all those who gaze on them.

AFTERNOONS IN THE PARK

I stumbled by accident upon this terrarium in a vast antiques/junk emporium. I had been searching for a gilt frame for another project and took a few minutes out to scour the aisles. Hidden behind an old red post-box was this colored glass terrarium. It had been neglected—in fact, most of the glass was missing   but I could see its potential. I had it repaired and removed the lower glass panels, but it was well worth the wait once it was fully restored. I just love the green glass because it works so well with the green moss.

I placed a miniature white park bench in the center of the moss and laid a small folded newspaper on the seat. I think they convey the idea of a summer afternoon spent relaxing in the park perfectly.

While wandering through a park, why not take a few moments to sit down and while away the afternoon with a newspaper?

CONTAINED **ABUNDANCE**

This large terrarium (shown opposite) needs plenty of space. It's quite an eye-catcher, being a heady combination of color and texture. The traditional shape and form of the terrarium reminds me of a Victorian garden room—very structured with large panes of glass. Here, I've gone for a complete contrast in the planting. Indeed, instead of adhering to clear lines and color blocks, as the shape of the terrarium would suggest, I've created a busy picture of moss and succulents, alongside the darker *Begonia* and *Fittonia* (nerve plant). It reminds me of a lost garden, a Victorian garden hidden on a country estate away from prying eyes.

Below: This terrarium called for a single plant with strong colors. I chose this lovely *Callistemon* (bottlebrush plant), with its striking bright pink flowers,

which I knew would be just right for this majestic house. This is such a striking terrarium and an arrangement such as this needs attention and pride of place in your home.

Delicate shades of pink and red serve to enhance the arrangements in these traditional glasshouses.

VICTORIAN EXHIBITION

This handsome assortment of dark bark and pale pebbles makes an arresting display for any corner of a room. The dark tones in the vintage terrarium remind me of a dark-hued Victorian gentleman's club from the 19th century, containing collected finds from a desert expedition. I discovered this terrarium in an antiques market and, after some polishing and careful cleaning, it looked just perfect for my shelf! The plants in the terrarium are *Tillandsia* (or air plants). (For further advice on how to grow and care for air plants, see page 112.)

To complete the scene, I added an interestingly shaped piece of wood and some reindeer moss, and then scattered the base of the terrarium with bark chips and a few pebbles.

This is one of my favorite terrarium displays, as it's so simple and elegant, while still having an air of luxury. The background and surroundings are so unassuming that they really allow the air plants to shine and stand out in all their regal exquisiteness. Encased in such a wonderful terrarium, these air plants would look just as good with only the bogwood as a simple pedestal.

These wonderfully exotic air plants call for careful scrutiny. Arranged with some wood and moss, this combination is a real show-stopper.

GREAT EXPECTATIONS

Welcome to the wonderful world of Miss Havisham: busy and vibrant, yet ethereal and gentle at the same time. The large size and antiquated appearance of this terrarium allows activity inside; it's a great opportunity to be creative. Inspired by one of my favorite and most intriguing literary characters—Charles Dickens' Miss Havisham from the classic novel *Great Expectations*—this terrarium is a celebration of her creative disorder. I started with the white roll-top bath, and placed small pieces of *Ajuga reptans* (bugleweed) and moss inside, so creating a sense of green neglect. I then built up the moss and busy green plants, which include maidenhair and boston ferns, along with *Fittonia* (nerve plant), around the bath. This terrarium is best placed in a sunny position. The final decorative piece is a beautiful tiny birdcage, a small reminder of Miss Havisham for the picture.

AQUATIC LANDSCAPE

Living in London, I often miss the pond at my parents' house. On a warm summer's day, it's so lovely to look at, watching the different fish and admiring the lush aquatic plants. So, I wanted to re-create this effect indoors. Aquatic plants are very much under-used in plant displays, which is a real shame as there are so many different and interesting plants to choose from. In fact, with a little imagination, you can create a real show-stopper! In this imaginative display, you're not only creating something green, but also making a small indoor pond in a beautiful glass vase.

For this display, I included a beautiful piece of dark-colored bark, which is called bogwood, a selection of water moss balls, which are created by the churning of underwater currents, and an *Echinodorus amazonicus* (Amazon sword plant). This is an aquatic plant that is happy to grow solely in water. I secured the plant in place by stitching it onto the piece of bark with some dark cotton. I still haven't decided whether to add some small fish... (For further advice on aquatic horticulture, see page 113.)

Bringing water displays indoors can have a calming effect, while being an interesting piece of decor.

LESS IS DEFINITELY MORE

Glass bell jars make a sizeable terrarium and, again, are easy to source from flea markets. Here I've kept the look simple and have not complicated the picture with too many busy plants. The leaves of the fern—here, I planted *Biophytum sensitivum*—take up most of the space and are similar in color to the lighter green of the moss. These plants prefer moist, well-drained potting mix and medium light.

Sometimes less is definitely more because, even though there is space for more plants, I wanted to keep the display as simple as possible. I also found some old mosaic tiles and carefully broke them up into smaller pieces—I think the cobalt blue of the mosaic really enhances the look. The tiny terracotta jar, containing a few small flowers cut from the garden, reminds me of an old Moroccan cooking pot, and finishes off the display perfectly.

A wonderfully tropical terrarium scene, with a splash of shocking pink, which is made all the better for its simplicity.

TIME FOR TEA

This narrow glass terrarium is simple, but effective; bottles and vases such as this are easy to find and, with a little imagination and flair, can be turned into something interesting. I knew I wanted a small plant for this terrarium and the small, delicate foliage of the succulent *Senecio Rowleyanus* 'String of Pearls' is a perfect match. Planted in some green moss, the succulent creates a focal point. I also found some small doll-sized pieces of porcelain china and gently lowered them into the bottle. I think this creates quite a restful look, reminding me of a relaxing afternoon tea.

A blue-and-white miniature tea set makes for interesting viewing in this unusual decanter terrarium.

ECHO OF THE SEA

These three vintage preserving jars are perfect for a kitchen display of indoor plants. Terrarium-style planters need not be expensive, since the plants don't need to be housed in antique cases or terrariums commissioned from a specialist maker. In fact, it's more fun to think outside the box and be imaginative. So, visit antiques stores, flower markets, and thrift shops, or look in your own home—are there any jars or vases that you've always kept but never found a use for?

I found these beautiful matching vintage jars while in America. They were produced during the 1920s and 1930s. As soon as I spotted them, I knew they would look great in my kitchen. I was almost tempted to use them for something else, but I have to admit that I was rather hesitant about storing food ingredients in a vintage jar, so I turned them into an innovative plant display instead.

When I found the jars I was on vacation close to the coast, so I have kept that holiday feeling and remind myself of the walks on the beach by using golden sand as a base for the plants. Succulents grow very well in sand; simply place a spoonful or two of succulent potting mix in the base of the jar, then sprinkle the sand around the sides and over the top to hide the potting mix. I used reindeer moss in all three jars and picked different glossy succulents, including *Crassula ovata* (jade or money plant), which is one of my favorites. Other succulents you could use include *Schlumbergera* (Christmas cactus), *Sempervivum tectorum* (common houseleek or, rather charmingly, hens-and-chicks), and *Kalanchoe tomentosa* (panda plant). Spend some time looking into your preferred succulents and thinking about which colors would work best in your own kitchen. Water your succulents sparingly.

Preserve special memories of
vacations by the sea by
keeping them in beautiful
mason jars.

A fun and inventive way of using old light bulbs in order to display seasonal cuttings from the garden.

A BRIGHT SPARK

For this arrangement I felt like doing a bit of DIY, so I went to repurpose some old light bulbs that I was storing under the stairs. After the light bulbs had gathered dust for a few months, I had a flash of interior inspiration after visiting an art exhibition in Stockholm and spotting some empty light bulbs in a stunning display. I knew the stark and industrial-looking light bulbs would make perfect modern, miniature terrariums; they also make a great contrast to the natural elements in the display. There are various ways to turn the light bulbs into miniature terrariums, and these techniques can all be found online. It can be rather fiddly, but I think it is well worth it. I used a plumbing ring, which I glued onto the base of each light bulb, to add stability.

The light bulbs make wonderful holders for cuttings and the stems of plants such as the white *Syringa vulgaris* (lilac) featured here. I also used white roses, a variegated variety of *Schefflera* (umbrella tree), and *Ficus benjamina* (weeping fig). You don't need to be too exact when choosing cuttings for display and can take anything from your garden that's in flower or looking attractive. Just aim to include a mix that you enjoy looking at. The light-bulb-factory look makes a great modern contrast to any overly pretty plants and flowers. It's also effective to mis-match the sizes of the light bulbs and the various cuttings.

A DAY IN THE COUNTRY

This beautiful Victorian terrarium is a favorite of mine because the stunning green panes and copper edges look wonderful together. It was a great vintage find and I've had lots of fun putting together the picture inside. I visited the doll house furniture shop for the miniature pieces, and decided I wanted to create a vision of a sunny summer afternoon spent outside. Even though the pretty pale blue *Campanula carpatica* is very small, it looks like a large, blooming bush here, conjuring up images of an English country garden. As a big fan of container gardening, I also jumped at the chance to feature a miniature pot in this terrarium—the tiny blue flower in the blue pot is *Myosotis scorpioides* (forget-me-not).

A GARDEN SCENE

The Victorians were particularly enthusiastic about building and creating their own terrariums, and it soon became fashionable for most homes to boast one sitting on a side table. People were quite imaginative about the plants and props they chose to place inside their terrariums, and so pieces of family memorabilia, china, and even jewelry were often displayed among the plants.

In this handsome steel-framed terrarium, I wanted to display a few fun artifacts, and create a garden picture. Using a selection of pale pebbles as a base, with some bright green cushion moss and an eye-catching *Nertera granadensis* (orange bead plant), I added miniature gardening tools and a tall birdbox to add height to the display. As a keen gardener, I thought that this would make a particularly fun terrarium for my home. Scour toy shops and look for doll house accessories to source your own terrarium props.

Bead plants do not produce many "beads" if there is insufficient light or if it's too warm. A cool, sunny position or a south-facing windowsill is ideal. Keep the potting mix moist throughout spring and summer, but allow it to dry out between waterings in fall and winter. Feed once a month in spring and summer with a soluble liquid fertilizer diluted to half strength until the plant begins to flower.

Dream of the gentle waters of an aquamarine pool lapping around your feet in an emerald-green paradise.

3

MOSS WALLS AND HANGING GARDENS

I love the idea of hanging plants indoors because you can really use your ingenuity and creativity here. In many ways, a hanging display also functions as a work of art because you are creating a stunning focal point in your home to show off your plants. Here, I have used a variety of hanging objects, from metal hanging baskets to recycled glass bottles—there really are no limitations to how you suspend your houseplants. My favorite projects use simple picture frames to house a selection of mosses and succulents and a stylish copper-edged holder against a neutral wall to display unusual air plants.

HANGING VINE

Hanging baskets can seem staid and fussy, with too many plants crowded into a small, often ugly basket. This beautiful metallic container breaks the rule, however, as it's both handsome and simple—great for a stylish bedroom or perhaps displayed at the top of a flight of stairs. The delicate, glossy leaves of the plant fall over the edge of the container, making for an easy, uncluttered look. In this display, I used *Pellaea rotundifolia*, which is commonly known as the button fern. A small, low-growing fern, it is easy to grow and creates a unique look with its small, rounded leaflets.

How wonderful to wake up to the sight of pretty leaves tumbling over the edges of a suspended glass container.

HANGING BOTTLES

For this creative project, I selected a trio of green-glass wine bottles. Recycling and re-using containers is a wonderful way to make the most of budget gardening. You really don't need very much—just some ingenuity to create a lovely green picture. (For detailed instructions on how to cut down and plant the wine bottles, see page 118.)

The lush greens and purples of the plants dripping out of the bottles work really well in a kitchen. They look great in any window, but particularly against the steel-framed window here, which is a lovely feature of this kitchen's pantry. The plants used are *Begonia foliosa* (fern begonia), *Hatiora salicornioides* (dancing bones cactus), and *Ficus benjamina* (weeping fig).

This unique and stylish way of recycling old bottles is perfect to display unusual plants in your home.

FIRESIDE MOSS

Walking down the high street in Hampstead, in London, one day, I was struck by a scene in one of the shop windows. Here lay a luscious carpet of moss and some cloches containing shoes. This got me thinking: why not have such "scenes" in your home? Houseplants don't need to be kept in traditional containers and you can definitely have fun creating scenes with different themes. I really love this particular display, as it's a real show-stopper that reminds me of a mysterious woodland landscape. It would also be a lovely way to showcase your houseplants when you have friends over for dinner, or just to please yourself.

To create the scene, I laid a lush carpet of mosses, using a mixture of bun, reindeer, and sheet moss, which I then interspersed with succulents to provide additional texture and interest.

I used a variety of succulents here, including *Sempervivum tectorum* (common houseleek or hens-and-chicks), *Echeveria elegans* (Mexican snowball), *Anacampseros rufescens*, *Jovibarba hirta* 'Andreas Smits', and *Echeveria* 'Imbricata', but any can be used for this display. The pieces of driftwood create a wonderfully earthy feel and are further enhanced by shells and more clumps of moss. The fireplace is the perfect spot for the display, while the glass cloches, housing tiny terracotta pots planted with more moss, create an air of illusion and mystery, suggesting that you may find hidden treasures nearby.

I also used three different kinds of fern, including *Dryopteris filix-mas* 'Linearis Polydactyla', a type of hardy fern, and a species of *Adiantum* (maidenhair fern), both of which I placed within the moss carpet. I put a *Cheilanthes lanosa* (hairy lip fern) in the fireplace. These ferns all add height and create the illusion of a forest—texture is really important in this display. Ferns are one of the oldest groups of plant and there are literally thousands of varieties. As houseplants, they make great air purifiers. They also bring a real "Jurassic Park" feel to this display. There are endless ways in which to embellish the scene, so let your imagination run riot and create your own secret garden.

Please note that this scene isn't a "forever" display, but you could contain the moss in trays, ensuring you water them regularly, if you wish to keep it for a couple of months.

A wealth of different textures, from smooth, shiny leaves to frond-like mosses and intricate succulents, creates a scene of gentle beauty.

TIME FOR REFLECTION

Houseplants are beneficial for so many reasons: they bring life, visual interest, and extra oxygen into your home. They can be characterful, adding an extra-special touch to your indoor space that just can't be attained using other items of home decoration. One of my favorite arrangements is this delicate wire container. It's perfect for a home office or reading corner, or perhaps next to a much-loved leather armchair. The dark mosses—here I used sphagnum moss—peeking out of the container boast a lovely, lush green color; they are also messy and slightly wild-looking. The tall, dark green plant, *Castanospermum australe* (blackbean), growing through the center of the moss makes a real impact, particularly when the container is placed on an antique side table or sideboard. The succulents planted at the foot of the feature plant are *Sedum rubrotinctum* (jelly bean plant). This small container adds instant life and brightness to a neglected corner. I lined the container with plastic sheeting to stop water leaking out, but you could use a plastic tray instead.

MOSS MASTERPIECE

This is a really fun display to create and one that you can get the kids involved in as well. I think there is a lot to be said for turning your garden into a sort of outdoor room that you can decorate in much the same way as you would a room indoors. It becomes a place where you can sit, look about you, and relax.

This is a simple project to set up and uses a rectangular piece of hardboard. I painted the hardboard white, but you can use any color you wish and perhaps take inspiration from the surrounding garden plants. I used eggshell paint, but gloss paint would work even better as the display will be exposed to the elements outdoors.

Take some reindeer moss—I have used three different shades of green here. You could even spray-paint some of the pieces of moss with different colors to create a more interesting scene. Use a hot glue gun to fix the moss to the hardboard. There is no right or wrong way to position the moss and, in fact, using different colors will mean you can be quite messy in your approach. This moss picture adds a lush feeling to the plain brick wall and brightens up a dark winter day!

With its striking combination of colors and textures, this painting of moss creates a stunning focal point on a garden wall.

FRAMED BRILLIANCE

This is one of those displays that is guaranteed to wow your visitors to your home; it's a really simple idea, but so striking! Here, I took three box picture frames and placed bun moss inside them. You need to keep the moss plants moist, so remember to spray them every day.

I also picked up this wonderful gilt frame from a flea market. It was while thinking up this display that it jumped into my mind, so I retrieved it from under the bed. I love the juxtaposition of the simple, modern, white frames with the ornate detail of the gold frame.

You will need to build a box behind the gilt frame. To do this, I used some pieces of wood, which I cut to size to make a box behind the frame in order to hold the *sempervivum* succulents. I then placed a piece of chicken wire over the top between the back of the picture frame and the top of the box and fixed it in place with a hot glue gun. The chicken wire will hold the succulents firmly in position. Fill the box with potting mix to a depth of approximately 1in (3cm). You then simply poke the succulents through the holes in the wire and fill all the space in the picture frame with them.

Allow a living wall of art to take center stage in a daring display, which exhibits a wealth of different textures.

A CREATIVE WALL

Tillandsia or air plants are such unusual plants but they are surprisingly easy to maintain, even though they look very different from the bright green plants we're used to growing in our homes. Air plants may be grown remotely in weird and wonderful spots—you can even grow them on other plants, on objects such as a pieces of wire, and even on the sides of buildings. Many people think air plants are rather strange-looking, but, if you are open-minded, they can make wonderful plants for stylish interiors. Indeed, these hanging pieces look stunning against the gray hues of the wall. The copper-edged holder, which houses its air plant so well and sets off the white ceramic pot beautifully, was a lucky find in a vintage store. This is a great display for a bare wall that desperately needs some interest. (For further advice on growing and caring for air plants, see page 112.)

The delicate details and soft hues of these air plants and holders add intrigue to a bare wall.

5

TOOLS, MATERIALS, AND TECHNIQUES

This may be your first foray into nurturing houseplants, or you may be a seasoned pro. Even so, most people need to look afresh at their houseplant displays now and then, so, although you may be using this book only as a source of inspirational ideas, I will cover the basics of growing houseplants from start to finish, as this is a book for both the beginner and the experienced gardener. The main requirements for growing healthy houseplants are a well-lit, draught-free spot with an even temperature and reasonably high humidity. However, some plants have specific needs, and this section will show you how to care for them.

TOP 10 HOUSE GARDENING TIPS

Here are a few useful guidelines to help you start growing plants in your home:

1 Position plants carefully Choose plants that suit the environment, as even the most dedicated gardener can't make a sun-loving plant thrive in a cold, shady area. So, ensure that your plants are suited to the light levels and temperature of the room in which they'll be positioned.

2 Try to avoid direct sun Windowsills in direct sunlight will be too hot for most houseplants. Also, don't place houseplants over direct sources of heat, such as radiators.

3 Avoid shady areas Ensure there is sufficient light for your houseplants to photosynthesize effectively.

4 Avoid temperature extremes Keep delicate plants away from draughts, as these will decrease humidity levels.

5 Pot on regularly Aim to repot your houseplants into larger pots every two years or so. This will ensure that they are not stressed and will thrive.

6 Be well equipped Use the proper tools for indoor gardening. A long-spouted watering can and a mister to increase humidity are both essential for reducing dust levels, as well as dealing with pest and disease outbreaks. A long-handled fork and a pair of scissors are great for accessing difficult areas, while a sponge attached to a long handle will keep glass containers clean.

7 Water wisely Don't overwater houseplants; adding some drainage material at the bottom of the pot will help to keep roots aerated and ensure that they don't drown.

8 Winter dormancy Allow houseplants to rest during the winter period and move them to a cooler position. This is because most plants are dormant at this time, and so don't need as much sunlight. You should also reduce the amount of water and food you provide, as this can help to prevent diseases such as mold and root rot. Move plants away from windows because these areas will be too cold in the winter.

9 Be vigilant Learn to recognize potential problems early on before a pest infestation or other physiological problems kill off your plant. For example, danger signs for low air humidity include flower buds falling off, leaves withering, and leaves with brown tips. Signs of high humidity include mold, rot, and soft growth.

10 Think long-term Some popular houseplant gifts only have a short growing period, so choose plants that will thrive for longer if you want a year-round display.

GETTING STARTED

Knowing a little about the processes by which plants live can be useful when growing and maintaining houseplants. Living indoors is not natural for plants, so it's essential you don't inhibit their growth by providing them with wrong growing conditions.

LIGHT LEVELS

Most houseplants, including orchids and bromeliads, thrive in filtered sunlight, but all-green-leaved plants such as philodendrons can live happily away from windows and even in the shade. However, variegated- and colored-leaved plants, flowering plants, and cacti and succulents must have good light levels to flower or do well.

TEMPERATURE

Every plant has a preferred temperature range in which it will grow well and it will die if exposed to temperatures outside this range for a long period of time. Central heating or a dry atmosphere can have detrimental effects, drying out and scorching your plants, so avoid placing them in direct sunlight or too near a radiator. You should also avoid extreme fluctuations in temperature, as this will shock the plant, with adverse effects. Draughts—such as those found on window ledges and near outside doors—will cause increased transpiration and rapidly dry out your plants. As a guide, bear the following ideal temperatures in mind when growing houseplants:

- The minimum winter temperature (and for winter dormancy) is 55°F (12°C).
- The average temperature for plants to thrive is 65–75°F (18–24°C).
- Plants from less tropical regions grow well in 50–60°F (10–16°C).
- Fluctuations of 20°F (11°C) or more within 24 hours are detrimental to all plants, so keep temperatures constant.
- Young seedlings will grow well in a constant temperature.

HUMIDITY

It is advisable to match the humidity levels to the plant; for example, cacti need a dry atmosphere. If you wish to raise humidity levels, try grouping plants together in one place. Regular misting will also help to increase humidity and aid plant growth.

LIGHT AND PHOTOSYNTHESIS

The process of photosynthesis provides plants with energy and occurs naturally as a result of the green pigment chlorophyll in their leaves and stems. (Plants such as cacti only have chlorophyll in their stems.) Sunlight acts on the chlorophyll to produce carbohydrates, using carbon dioxide from the air and water from the soil. The carbon dioxide is taken in by stomata (or pores) that are usually found on the underside of the leaves. The light energy splits the water molecules into oxygen and hydrogen. The hydrogen combines with the carbon to produce carbohydrates like glucose that provide the plant with food. Oxygen and water vapor are released into the air as by-products of the process, which is why plants are so beneficial to us indoors.

CHOOSING AND POSITIONING CONTAINERS

When choosing a container for your houseplant, the most important consideration is to ensure that your plant and pot are in proportion. Your choice will inevitably be influenced by personal preference, but you should also take the time to check that the container will work aesthetically where you are going to position it.

TYPES OF CONTAINER

Your new houseplant will normally come in a plastic pot, unless you are buying one that has already been planted up in its "smart" container. This is where you can choose a container that reflects your personal style and surroundings. It is very important to check that the container has holes at the bottom so that water can drain away and so prevent the plant from rotting. Also, if you are grouping plants together, make sure that the containers match and preferably group them in odd numbers to enhance the aesthetics of the arrangement. I tend to use simple pots; that is, nothing too fussy and highly patterned, as I feel this detracts from the impact of the plant.

Terrariums

Terrariums are great for growing indoor plants in today's centrally heated and air-conditioned homes. Growing plants in a closed glass case, or terrarium, means that water evaporating from the leaves during transpiration condenses on the glass and then trickles down the sides of the case to be reabsorbed by the roots.

Unlike their Victorian predecessors, terrariums today are both affordable and suitable for smaller houses and apartments. They are a wonderful way to keep succulents and cacti indoors, preventing them from rotting or drying out. Easy to create, they make a great project for the whole family.

You'll need to decide whether you would like your terrarium to be open or closed. Open terrariums can tolerate some direct sunlight, but be aware that too much sun may burn any leaves that are in direct contact with the sides of the terrarium. In contrast, closed terrariums need a location where they will receive bright light, but no direct sunlight. If they are placed in direct sunlight, the temperature inside the terrarium can rise considerably and "cook" the plants. (A closed terrarium may also be an open terrarium that has a cover.)

Whether you opt for an open or closed terrarium should also be determined by your choice of plants—sun-loving plants yearn for natural light, so use an open terrarium, while plants that require high levels of humidity need a closed terrarium. Mind-your-own-business (Soleirolia soleirolii), violas, mosses, and cacti and succulents will all grow well in a terrarium.

Glass vases

It is unusual to grow plants in potting mix in a glass container, as their roots don't fare well when exposed to the light. However, they make great receptacles for creating water gardens and growing aquatic plants. Adding some pebbles helps to reduce the light levels and so these are widely used in glass containers.

Clay containers

Containers made from clay or terracotta can prove both practical and versatile when you're growing houseplants. You can choose terracotta pots in their natural color or paint them to blend in with your décor or environment. Because terracotta is a porous material, the pots lose water from their sides, as well as from the base, so may need watering more frequently. Using a decorative mulch or topping can help to reduce excess evaporation.

Wooden crates

A wooden crate makes a great partner for lush foliage plants and can be kept natural or painted to match your environment. Wood is not watertight, however, so you will also need to give the crate a plastic lining. Be careful when watering, though, because you don't want the plants' roots to become waterlogged. Alternatively, you can make a few holes in the base of the crate to allow excess water to escape, but take care that draining water doesn't cause any damage to the surface the crate sits on.

Hanging objects

Even if space is at a premium, you can still introduce interesting foliage into your home by using hanging objects as containers. They can also make a striking focal point in a room.

Window boxes

A window box is a great way to use up space on your window ledges, both inside and out. Choose boxes that complement your space.

Handmade objects

You will derive a great deal of pride and pleasure from making your own containers, whether you are just re-using household items or making them from scratch. I have used a variety of handmade objects in the book, so look through the projects to see if you feel there are any you would enjoy making yourself.

TIP

Ceramic pots and saucers can sometimes damage surfaces, so stick on a felt, latex (rubber), or foam pad square to protect your furniture.

TERRARIUMS–A BRIEF HISTORY

In 1827, a London doctor called Nathaniel Ward created a terrarium by accident while building a fern rockery. Ward found that his plants kept dying because of poisoning by heavy fumes from London's factories. He was also studying moths and caterpillars, keeping several insects in covered jars so that he could observe their behavior. Ward placed several plants, including some of the rockery ferns, alongside the cocoons. He noticed that the plants were healthy and grew well in the hot conditions under the enclosed glass, and came to the conclusion that plants could flourish in London if protected from the city's polluted air.

Ward spent years experimenting with miniature greenhouses and planting indoors, and eventually developed the Wardian case or terrarium. It was an exciting discovery for horticulturalists who were able to bring back sensitive tropical plants in Wardian cases that kept them well protected from salty air and changing climatic conditions during long sea voyages. Wardian cases became popular with fashionable households and it was trendy to keep one in your front room. They grew into miniature Taj Mahals and Brighton Pavilions, and were a wonderful way for Victorians to display decorative objects beside living plants.

China and porcelain containers

These are available in a vast array of shapes and sizes, as well as lots of different colors and designs. When designing a container grouping, I usually make sure that the containers complement one another in all of these areas. Using lots of different patterns, colors, and textures not only makes a display look messy and old-fashioned, but can also distract your attention away from the plants. China and porcelain containers are unlikely to have drainage holes, so make sure you remove any excess water after watering.

Metal containers and wire crates

Containers made from metal are wonderfully contemporary and also a great way to recycle unusual objects. Few have drainage holes, but you can easily make these yourself using a drill and drill bit or a hammer and strong nail.

GROUPING CONTAINERS

If you decide to group containers together, make sure the pots match or are of the same design or style. Also, consider your choice of plants carefully and think about whether they will look attractive with the pot. A good way to check this before potting up is to place the plant behind the pot and then stand back to see the effect.

When you choose containers for grouping, another useful design concept is to make sure that you have an odd number of planters, so aim for container groups of 3, 5, or 7.

Try to think outside the box and be creative. Indeed, throughout this book, I have used lots of recycled objects that are not technically for plants, but are a great way to create an interesting focal point.

There are two main principles for arranging containers: you can either have a symmetrical arrangement with one large container and two smaller ones on either side, or you can make the arrangement asymmetrical by positioning both smaller containers on one side of a larger one.

TOOLS AND MATERIALS

The tools and materials you use are really important when caring for and maintaining your houseplants. You don't need to spend a fortune, however, as many tools can be made from household spoons, forks, and knives with a bit of tape and a long stick. Here, I have outlined the most useful tools for all the projects in the book.

USEFUL TOOLS

Mini spades or trowels for digging holes and moving objects in containers.

Mini rake for raking over and patting down the potting mix.

Sticks are great for moving and positioning plants in difficult areas and also for putting holes in the potting mix when you are sowing seeds.

Stiff paper for making a funnel to pour materials into small, difficult-to-access containers.

Long-handled tweezers are useful for grabbing plants when you're positioning them in small containers.

A magnifying glass is helpful for enlarging small objects when planting up a terrarium.

Scissors are one of the most useful tools, as you will find them really helpful for deadheading, trimming back, tidying up, pruning, and taking cuttings.

Long-handled scissors are great for pruning and tweaking off dead leaves.

Leaf pruners are really useful for cutting more woody and mature plant stems that cannot be cut with a pair of scissors.

Root clippers are a great tool when you're repotting plants (especially bonsai) and also for propagating plants by division.

Homemade glass cleaner for cleaning areas difficult-to-reach areas inside pots, glass vases, and terrariums. To make your own, simply stick a small sponge onto the end of a chopstick.

Small brushes are useful for brushing stray potting mix from plant leaves.

Bamboo sticks and trellis are ideal for providing plants such as climbers with a form of support, and for training plants.

Wire for training plants, such as Passiflora (passionflower) and Hedera (ivy), as well as for tying in untidy branches. A good green-coated floristry wire is perfect, as the green will blend in with the plant.

Floristry pins are great for holding down mosses and fixing parts of clump moss together. A ball of string is useful for securing climbing plants and fixing moss around the plant.

Plant labels are helpful when sowing different seeds, so you can remember what they are. Spray bottles can be used for misting plants, as well as for treating pests with pesticides and fungicides.

Below from left to right: A selection of tools: scissors, magnifying glass, mini rake, glass cleaner, small brush, long-handled tweezers, bamboo stick, floristry pins and wire, long-handled scissors, mini spade, mini trowel.

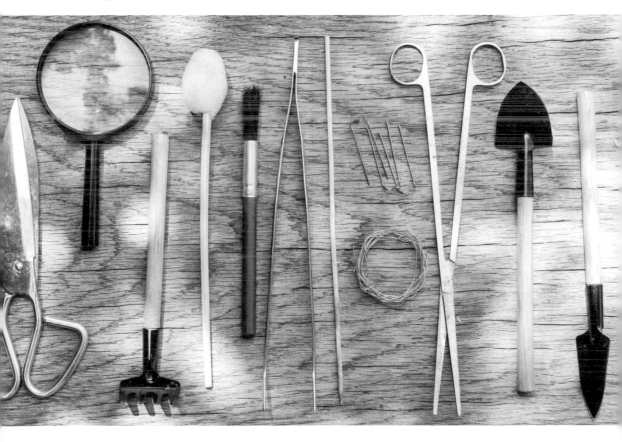

POTTING MIXES

Most indoor plants will thrive in sterile, soil-less potting mix (either peat- or peat-substitute-based). It is not recommended that you use garden soil, as it may contain weed seeds or diseases. Potting mix is sterile and does not contain any fungi, weeds, pests, soil-borne diseases, seeds, or toxins to prevent your plants from growing well.

Specialty potting mixes are also available for particular plants with specific needs, including ericaceous potting mix for lime-hating plants, such as camellias, and gritty, fast-draining potting mix for cacti. Coarse, low-nutrient potting mixes, which contain vermiculite and perlite, are ideal for orchids. This is because orchids are particularly sensitive and don't like getting their roots wet. You can use a seedling potting mix for sowing seeds and growing seedlings.

DECORATIVE TOPPINGS

Using a decorative topping not only finishes off your container aesthetically, but also helps the plant to retain moisture. You will need to move the decorative topping aside slightly when checking if your plant needs watering. I have listed my favorites below, but again, it's a case of personal choice—just remember to match the topping to your container and its surroundings.

Moss is ideal for top-dressing container plantings and there are many different varieties to choose from. Reindeer moss is wonderful used in combination with sand toppings. Spaghnum moss is perfect for covering the potting mix in terrariums. Fern or sheet moss makes a great cover for large-scale planters owing to its size. Water moss balls, which are produced by the churning of rivers, are spherical balls of moss that look striking in water terrariums. Pillow moss —often known as clump or cushion moss—forms neat clumps, which range from small, round mounds to larger, irregularly shaped mounds. Pillow moss is great for making miniature gardens because it looks like rolling fields.

Sand looks lovely on simple story gardens and is particularly nice to use when you're planting up a container as a project with children. I like to use aquatic sands because they give a finer finish and are available in a multitude of colors.

Pebbles are available in various shapes, sizes, and finishes from garden and aquatic centers.

Woodchips are perfect for arrangements that have a more natural, earthy feel.

Fine gravel is great for giving a more organic feel to your planting display.

Shells can be great fun to find on the beach. I pick up many different shells on my trips to the seaside.

Slate chips works well with sleek, modern arrangements.

TIPS ON GROWING MOSS

- It is possible to grow moss on a tray. Take some samples of moss from roofs and pavements. Divide the moss into squares measuring approximately 1½–2in (4–5cm), and place these pieces on a layer of well-watered potting mix. Moss takes quite a while to grow, but growing your own means you can use different types that aren't readily available from floristry suppliers.
- Soak the moss well with water. It can be stored in the refrigerator or freezer if you don't need to use all of it at once.
- Mosses need to be kept moist at all times to grow and retain their lush green color.

BASIC TECHNIQUES

When choosing an indoor plant, it's worth doing some research to find out what position it will thrive in best, the growing conditions it needs, and whether it will fit in with the intended environment. This will ensure that your plant remains healthy and you can avoid making costly mistakes.

SELECTING A HEALTHY PLANT

When buying a houseplant from a garden center or nursery, take the time to check that you have chosen a healthy specimen that will thrive once you get home. The following checklist should help you to make a good choice:

• Look for strong, healthy leaves with a good vibrant color. Avoid any plant with damaged or blotchy leaves.

• The plant's stems should be firm and, if the plant is flowering, choose one that has lots of unopened buds for a longer flowering period.

• Check that there is no space between the potting mix and the inside of the pot, because this means the plant is extremely dry and will grow poorly.

• Make sure there are no insects or larvae on the plant; you don't want to introduce pest infestations into your home, as these may affect other houseplants.

• Avoid diseased plants with a furry mold at the base or any unsightly blotches.

• Check for any curled or withered leaves, which indicate that the plant won't grow well in future.

• Check that there are no soggy, wilted patches since this suggests that the plant has root rot or is pot-bound.

• Check that the roots are not growing out of the bottom of the pot. This means that the plant is pot-bound and so has been under stress.

• Buy a younger plant if possible because, although they are smaller, they'll adapt to their new environment better.

• When taking your plant home, make sure it is wrapped properly, as this will ensure that there is no damage to the leaves during transit.

• Don't place the plant in direct sunlight for the first few weeks, so that it can acclimatize before you move it to its final position. However, if you are buying a flowering plant, such as a cyclamen, azalea, or chrysanthemum, place it in its final sunny position immediately.

PLANTING A CONTAINER

There will be times when you need to pot up a plant, especially if you purchase it in an ugly plastic container. You may also need to repot a plant in order to give it a new lease of life or when it has outgrown its container.

1 Cover the bottom of the container with a layer of drainage material, such as gravel or pebbles, aiming to fill about a quarter of the container's volume. This will allow the roots to breathe and prevent them from drowning.

2 Fill the container with potting mix to bring the plant up so that the top of the root-ball is just beneath the rim of the container. Try to position the plant centrally in the container and make sure it is not lopsided.

3 Carefully feed more potting mix in between the plant and container, and firm it down. Avoid compacting the potting mix too much, though, as this will hinder drainage.

4 Add a layer of decorative mulch, such as fine gravel or shells, to finish off the planting. Not only does this make the container look more attractive, but it can also help to reduce the rate of evaporation.

GROWING AIR PLANTS

Tillandsias are a type of epiphyte, which is a plant that grows non-parasitically on another plant such as a tree. Often known as air plants, tillandsias also sometimes grow on other objects such as buildings or telegraph wires. They derive their moisture and nutrients from the air and rain, and also sometimes from any debris that accumulates around them. The roots are used only as anchors.

You can easily house air plants in hanging containers or interesting wall pots, or you could attach them to bark, as shown in the Victorian Exhibition display (page 54). To do this, I use a waterproof adhesive, although you can also use a hot glue gun if you have one, which is by far the fastest method. It is quite safe to attach the air plants to the bark after the glue has cooled down for a few seconds. The plants can be mounted at any time of the year and the roots will grow when conditions are optimum—ideally, a warm day with high humidity. Mist your air plants regularly in order to keep humidity levels high.

AQUATIC HORTICULTURE

Aquatic plants are those that have adapted to living in water or very waterlogged soil. The most common aquatic plants are *Taxiphyllum barbieri* (Java moss), *Bacopa caroliniana* (water hyssop), *Ceratophyllum* (hornwort), *Hydrocotyle leucocephala* (Brazilian pennywort), and *Hygrophila difformis* (water wisteria), all of which can easily be found in aquatic shops.

The plants may be secured in a water display in a number of different ways. For example, in the Aquatic Landscape display on page 58, I stitched the plants onto the bark with some dark cotton thread, while in Aquatic Dream, on page 48, I simply weighed down the plants with some large pebbles.

If you are growing plants in this way, you will need to change the water regularly, especially when it starts to get murky. I usually add two aspirins to the water in order to aid the plants' growth and prevent a build-up of bacteria. Also, bear in mind that algae growing on tank walls or on plant leaves will compete with the plants for light. You can remove the algae manually by scrubbing or scraping the walls of the tank weekly when you're changing the water and by rubbing the leaves gently between your fingers.

Another area of aquatic horticulture, often referred to as hydroculture, is the growing of ordinary plants in a soil-less medium or an aquatic-based environment—the plant takes its nutrients from the water. The roots of the plant might be anchored in clay aggregate and pebbles. Plants commonly grown in this way include *Tradescantia fluminensis* 'Albovittata' and *Cyperus alternifolius* (umbrella plant), and many bulbs, such as hyacinths.

GROWING PLANTS IN A TERRARIUM

A few simple guidelines should be followed when selecting a terrarium container: it must be made from glass or another clear material through which light can pass; there should be a large enough opening to allow you to add potting mix and plants; and the plants you select should all have similar environmental needs.

The basics of terrarium horticulture are easy. Once you've found a suitable terrarium container, make sure you clean it thoroughly before use to prevent bacteria growing inside. Place some rocks at the bottom for drainage, and add a layer of charcoal and clay pellets. I usually add these using a funnel made from a piece of strong card, as terrariums often have only small openings. The charcoal and clay pellets are important because they help to reduce excess moisture and the build-up of molds, odors, and fungus, keeping the terrarium environment healthy. This is because the charcoal acts as a purifier: as the water cycles through the terrarium, it is cleansed by the carbon in the charcoal. You can then add the potting mix and, finally, the plants. You may also include a few decorations if you wish. There are lots of different ways to present your indoor garden and make it look extra special.

1 Put a layer of clay gravel, about 1¼in (3cm) deep, at the bottom of the terrarium. Add a layer of charcoal, approximately ½–¾in (1–2cm) deep, on top of the clay gravel.

2 Fill the terrarium with approximately 2–2¼in (5–6cm) of potting mix. Use a mini trowel to smooth out the potting mix and make a hole for each of the plants.

3 Take your chosen plants—here I have used some camomile in order to make a miniature camomile lawn. You can use either a pair of long-handled tweezers or a fork to position the plants in their holes. Firm down the plants to anchor them securely in the potting mix. Pat down the exposed potting mix with a flat-topped fork.

4 Take some sheet moss and break off a piece to the size needed to cover the exposed potting mix. Take the flat-topped fork and gently firm down the moss.

5 Use a spray bottle to water the terrarium. It's best to spray, rather than use a watering can, because terrarium plants tend to be delicate. Spraying will also help to increase humidity levels, which the plants love.

6 Use a long-handled sponge to clean any dirt and debris from the sides of the terrarium.

7 Select a miniature object to create a story for your terrarium. Here, I have opted for a quirky feel and used a bicycle.

8 Use a brush to remove any stray specks of potting mix and ensure your terrarium is spotlessly clean.

9 Position your terrarium where you can enjoy it—the sleeping dog is optional!

GROWING PLANTS IN A HANGING BOTTLE

I really enjoy re-using objects, and this a wonderful way to convert some old wine bottles into a lovely plant display (see page 76). I love the look of the dark green glass with the purple and green leaves. Once the plants are firmly fixed in the bottles, you will need to water them once a week. To do this, carefully pour a steady stream of water through the neck of the bottle to dampen the potting mix and moss.

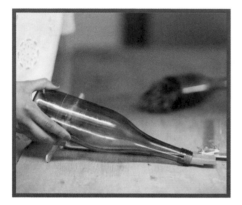

1 To create a hanging bottle, carefully score the bottle with a bottle cutter. (It is advisable to wear protective gloves and safety goggles when doing this.)

2 Run hot water over the scored part of the bottle, followed immediately by cold water.

3 Pour more hot water over the glass and the end of the bottle should break off. Use sandpaper to smooth the cut. You could use the bottom part as a little bowl for trinkets.

4 Remove your chosen plant from its container and neatly secure the root-ball with moss and pieces of wire in order to create a compact ball that will fit inside the bottom of the bottle. Attach two pieces of wire to the root-ball, ensuring that they are long enough for you to thread them through the bottle ready for hanging.

5 Carefully thread the two long wires through the bottle, taking care not to damage the leaves of the plant.

6 Repeat the process for each bottle and then suspend the bottles from the ceiling. Suspending the bottles at different levels makes for a more eye-catching display.

PLANT CARE

Although plants can withstand fluctuations in their growing conditions for a while, consistent care is essential for the health of your plants. Succulents, with their reserves, for example, can tolerate a little neglect more readily than a seedling, which has nothing to draw on.

HOW TO WATER

You should water plants more in spring and summer when they are actively growing and less when they are resting in winter. You can check whether a plant needs to be watered by pushing your fingers into the surface of the potting mix to a depth of about ½in (1cm). If the mix is not moist, then the plant needs to be watered.

There are two ways to water. You can water from above, which is the most convenient method and ensures an even distribution of water. Make sure there is a lip of about 1–1½in (2–3cm) between the potting mix and the top of the pot. This will allow the maximum amount of water to reach the plant. Alternatively, you can water from below, which involves watering the saucer to avoid wetting the crown of the plant and causing it to rot. This is particularly useful for fleshy plants such as cyclamen.

BOOSTING LIGHT LEVELS

Light levels can be increased by keeping the leaves of your plants clean, so allowing the maximum amount of light to be absorbed. Use a damp cloth or sponge-stick to wipe away dirt and other residues. Use a soft brush to clean away dust gently; this is particularly useful for cacti as you can get in between the spines.

STEM AND LEAF CUTTINGS

Taking a cutting involves removing a piece of the parent plant, such as a leaf stem or root, in order to grow a new plant. Taking cuttings is called vegetative propagation, and is the easiest method of propagating plants.

• **Stem cuttings:** Some plants, such as crassulas, azaleas, and camellias, are easier to propagate from stem cuttings than others and the cutting needs only to be placed in water to produce roots. Others will need a little help from a hormone-rooting powder to re-root. Propagation by stem cuttings is the most commonly used method to propagate many woody ornamental plants. Stem cuttings from many of my favorite shrubs are quite easy to root, although stem cuttings from tree species are usually more difficult to root.

In general, you should take cuttings from the current or past season's growth. Avoid material with flower buds if possible. Remove any flowers and flower buds when you are preparing a cutting so that the cutting's energy can be used to produce new roots rather than flowers. Take cuttings from healthy, disease-free plants, preferably from the upper part of the plant.

Suitable plants: *Crassula, Camellia, Epipremnum aurum* (devil's ivy), and *Hedera* (ivy).

• **Leaf cuttings:** Part-leaf cutting involves cutting a leaf along its length by the central vein and then placing the leaf lengthwise in some potting mix. New shoots should pop up along the cut. Once the cuttings are established, they can be transplanted to new pots. A whole-leaf cutting is where a whole leaf with a stem attached—perhaps from a succulent—is removed and the end pushed into some moist potting mix. New shoots should appear from the stem of the parent plant—these are called offsets.

Suitable plants: *Streptocarpus, Sedum, Sansevieria, Eucomis, Crassula*, and *Begonia masoniana*.

Offsets

Offsets should not be separated from the parent plant until they are well established. When the offsets resemble the parent plant in form and shape, separate them by using a knife to cut as close to the parent plant as possible. The offsets can then be repotted in some moist potting mix.

Suitable plants: Cacti and succulents.

DIVISION

Sansevierias, ferns, cacti, and orchids all have a clump of roots that can easily be divided to produce more plants. The new plants can then be planted up in individual pots. Simply select a point where you want to divide the plant and use a knife to separate the root-ball carefully. Make sure that you don't cause any damage, as this will affect the plant's roots and it may die.

Suitable plants: *Sansevieria, Hedera* (ivy), *Soleirolia soleirolii* (mind-your-own-business).

GRAFTING

Grafting, or hybridization, is a particularly useful method of propagation for cacti. This is where you take one part of a cactus and graft it onto another cactus to create a more interesting formation. To graft a cactus, use a knife to cut a V-shaped groove in the base plant. Replicate this in the graft with a pointed V so that it will fit inside the groove. Take a cocktail stick or a piece of wire and drive it vertically through the two plants to secure the two together.

Suitable plants: Cacti and succulents.

HANDLING DIFFICULT PLANTS

The following method is a great way to handle prickly plants such as cacti and ones that produce an irritable sap. Take a piece of folded newspaper or cloth, wrap it around the plant, and then use it as a handle while you knock the plant out of the upturned pot. Keep the newspaper in place while you position the plant in its new pot and until you have firmed in some fresh potting mix around the plant. Remove the "handle" once the plant is firmly in place.

CARING FOR CACTI AND SUCCULENTS

Desert cacti and succulents like a warm, sunny location where they will receive around four to six hours of warm sunlight every day. Place cacti in the sunniest spot in your home, perhaps on a windowsill or a table close to a window. Please note that forest cacti, such as *Schlumbergera* (Christmas cactus), will need some shade and less intense heat than desert cacti in summer, as well as a potting mix rich in organic matter and a little humidity.

• **Potting mix:** Use a potting mix specially formulated for cacti and succulents with added gravel and sand.

• **Watering:** Water cacti and succulents as needed—about once a month. A good indication that your cacti need watering is to lift the pot and see how heavy it is. If the pot feels lighter than usual, it's time to water your plant.

• **Feeding:** Feed cacti with a houseplant fertilizer that is high in nitrates and phosphorus. Feed once or twice a year, diluting the fertilizer to half the manufacturer's recommended amount.

• **Handling cacti:** Always use a strip of newspaper or card when handling cacti to avoid pricking your fingers (see page 124).

RESOURCES

UK

The Balcony Gardener
www.thebalconygardener.com
The Balcony Gardener team are
experts in small space gardening

Anthropologie
Stores across the United Kingdom
www.anthropologie.com/en-gb/
Garden accessories and homeware

Etsy
www.etsy.com
Quirky container finds to house your
plants, plus terrarium kits

IKEA
Stores across the United Kingdom
+44 (0)20 3645 0000
www.ikea.co.uk
Accessories, plant pots, and glassware

USA AND CANADA

Anthropologie
Stores across the United States
+1 (800) 309 2500
www.anthropologie.com
Ornate garden accessories
and homeware

Ben Wolff Pottery
Connecticut
+1 (860) 480 7765
www.benwolffpottery.com
Traditional and modern pottery

GRDN
Brooklyn, New York
+1 (718) 797 3628
www.grdnbklyn.com
A complete shop for the
urban gardener

Jayson
Chicago, Illinois
+1 (800) 472 1885
www.jaysonhome.com
Reclaimed pots and planters, plants,
and container planting

Pottery Barn
Stores across the United States
+1 (888) 779 5176
www.potterybarn.com
Outdoor lighting, garden furniture,
and outdoor tableware

Rolling Greens
Culver City, Los Angeles and Studio
City, California
+1 (310) 559 8656, +1 (323) 934 4500
or +1 (818) 432 7750
rghomeandgarden.com
Plants and containers

Sprout Home
Chicago, Illinois
(312) 226 5950
www.sprouthome.com
Contemporary garden accessories

Terrain
Glen Mills and Devon, Pennsylvania,
and Westport, Connecticut
+1 (877) 583 7724
www.shopterrain.com
Assortment of stylish garden supplies

West Elm
Stores across the United States
+1 (888) 922 4119
www.westelm.com
Containers and terrariums

ACKNOWLEDGMENTS

First of all, a huge, heartfelt thank you to Cindy, Sally, Gillian, and all the team at CICO Books for your belief in me, together with your guidance and patience in helping me create a book that I'm truly proud of. Thank you Helen for your amazing photography and Marisa for your beautiful styling—the results of your hard work are plain for all to see. Last but by no means least, a very, very special thank you to my fabulous, kind, and patient partner Luke for all your support and input, I couldn't have done any of this without you, especially the time you set aside to read and re-read my early drafts, to giving me advice on the cover, and particularly for your keeping the children busy and engaged so I could edit. You have been as important to this book reaching completion as I have. And finally, thanks to my wonderful family—my children, Jack and Elodie, my wonderful parents, Grandfather Bryan, Nick, and Uncle Mike—your continued support throughout is so appreciated and I will be forever indebted.

INDEX